Saved by the Alphabet

Written by
Maurice Prater

Illustrated by
Jason Koltuniak

Nihil Obstat and Imprimatur
The Most Reverend Peter J. Jugis, J.C.D.
Bishop of Charlotte

Divine Providence Press

Published by Divine Providence Press
c/o Dr. Joshua Hren, Ph.D.
506 Belmont Mt. Holly Road
Belmont, NC 28012

Divine Providence Press is an imprint of Wiseblood Books.
www.wisebloodbooks.com and www.divineprovidencepress.com

Ordering Information
E-Mail: wisebloodbooks@gmail.com
Phone: (314) 599-3627

Library of Congress Cataloging-in-Publication Data

Saved by the Alphabet / Maurice Prater
1. Prater, Maurice, 1962
2. Children's Book
3. Scriptural Alphabet Book

ISBN-13: 978-0-692-08222-5   ISBN-10: 0-692-08222-0

Scripture references are taken from *The Holy Bible: Douay-Rheims Version.*

Divine Providence Press works to spread the fragrance of Christ throughout the world, scattering little petals of providence by means of spiritual classics, devotional literature, children's books, and other writings that incarnate God's beauty and the splendor of truth.

Printed in the United States of America.

Dedication

Hail Mary, Full of Grace,	Luke 1:28
Mother of Jesus Christ,	Luke 1:31
And Mother of All Believers,	Apocalypse (Revelation) 12:17
Help Me to Love You as Jesus Loves You,	Luke 1:46-49
And in Return, Love Him as Only You Can.	Luke 1:38 and John 2:5

"And a great sign appeared in heaven: A woman clothed with the sun, and the moon under her feet, and on her head a crown of twelve stars."

Apocalypse (Revelation) 12:1

+JMJ+

Also available from Divine Providence Press:

Counting on Faith
A Scriptural Counting Book for Children

Do you know your ABCs?
Let's give it a try!

A is for Adam and Eve, the first man and first woman created by God.

B is for Boaz, who was kind to strangers, and who was the great-grandfather of King David.

C is for Christ Jesus, the Son of God, who died and rose from the dead to save us from our sins.

D

D is for Deborah, a brave judge of Israel and a military leader.

E is for Elijah the prophet,
who was taken up into Heaven by a whirlwind.

F is for Father, Son, and Holy Spirit,
also known as the Holy Trinity.

G is for God, Our Father, who created the world, and who is revealed in all of His creation.

H is for the Holy Family of
Jesus, Mary, and Joseph.

I is for Isaac, whose father Abraham led him up to the top of Mount Moriah, where they offered a sacrifice to God.

J is for Joseph the carpenter, husband of the Virgin Mary and foster father of Jesus.

K is for King David, who defeated the
giant Goliath and united his people.

L is for Luke, who wrote the third Gospel, or book of the Bible, about Jesus.

M is for Moses the prophet, who received the 10 Commandments from God.

N is for Noah, who built an Ark to save his family, including animals, from a flood.

O is for Onesimus (Oh-ness-uh-muss),
a friend who visited the apostle Paul in prison.

P is for Peter the apostle, to whom Jesus gave the keys to the Kingdom of Heaven.

Q is for Queen Esther, who protected the Jewish people living in Persia.

R is for Raphael, an angel of God
who helped Tobias heal his father's eyes.

S is for Susanna, Joanna, and Mary Magdalene,
who supported Jesus in His ministry.

T is for Timothy and Titus,
missionaries sent by the apostle Paul
to proclaim the Gospel of Jesus.

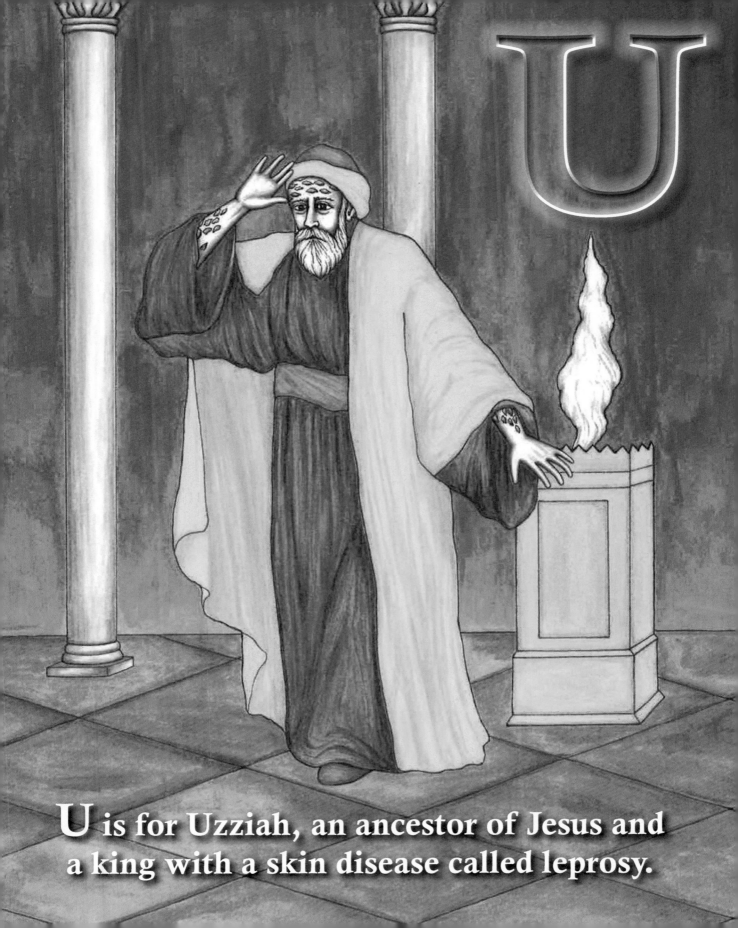

U is for Uzziah, an ancestor of Jesus and a king with a skin disease called leprosy.

V is for Virgin Mary, the mother of our brother and Savior Jesus Christ, and the mother of all believers.

W is for Wise Men, who brought gifts
to Jesus when He was born.

X is for Xerxes (zerk-sees), a Persian king who
helped Queen Esther protect the Jewish people.

Y is for You. Yes, you! Jesus said,
"Love one another as I love *you*."

Z is for Zechariah and Elizabeth, whose son John the Baptist was foretold by the angel Gabriel.

Now you know your ABCs!
God bless you!

Scriptural References

All scriptural references are from *The Holy Bible: Douay-Rheims Version.*

Letter A   Genesis 2:1-25

Letter B   Book of Ruth and Matthew 1:5-6

Letter C   Luke 1:26-38, Acts 5:27-32, and 1 Corinthians 15:1-8

Letter D   Judges 4:1 – 5:31

Letter E   4 Kings (2 Kings) 2:1-12 and Ecclesiasticus (Sirach) 48:1-16

Letter F   Matthew 28:16-20

Letter G   Genesis 1:1 – 2:3, Romans 1:19-20, and Ephesians 1:1-6

Letter H   Matthew 1:15-25 and Luke 1:26-38

Letter I   Genesis 22:1-19

Letter J   Isaiah 7:14, Matthew 1:15-25, and Luke 2:41-52

Letter K   1 Kings (1 Samuel) 17:1-58 and 2 Kings (2 Samuel) 5:1-5

Letter L   Gospel According to Luke

Letter M   Deuteronomy 5:1-22

Letter N   Genesis 6:5 – 9:17

Letter O   Colossians 4:7-9 and Letter to Philemon

Letter P   Matthew 16:13-20

Letter Q   Esther 2:5 – 9:32

Letter R   Tobias (Tobit) 11:1 – 12:22

Letter S   Luke 8:1-3

Letter T   First Letter to Timothy, Second Letter to Timothy, and Letter to Titus

Letter U   2 Paralipomenon (2 Chronicles) 26:1-22 and Matthew 1:8-9

Letter V   Luke 1:26 – 2:7, Hebrews 2:11-18, and Apocalypse (Revelation) 11:19 – 12:17

Letter W   Matthew 2:1-12 (Wise Men or "Magi")

Letter X   Book of Esther (Xerxes is also known as "Assuerus" or "Ahasuerus.")

Letter Y   John 15:11-17

Letter Z   Luke 1:5-25 and Luke 1:57-80